# Dr. Cookie's Cookbook

## NUTRITIOUS, DELICIOUS

## GOURMET COOKIES

## AND OTHER TREATS

Marvin A. Wayne, M.D., F.A.C.E.P.

SO-CYD-646

© Marvin A. Wayne, 1988

LIBERTY PUBLISHING COMPANY
Deerfield Beach, Florida

Published by:
**Liberty Publishing Company, Inc.**
440 South Federal Highway
Deerfield Beach, Florida 33441

Library of Congress #87-83149
ISBN 0-89709-165-5

Cover Photo: Torr Ofteness

Manufactured USA

*To*
*Joan, Michelle and Dana*
*who have shared my dream*
*of*
*"The Perfect Cookie"*

# Table of Contents

## Carob Collection

## Assortments

## BROWNIES AND FRUIT BARS

## QUICK BREADS

Send a friend a copy of this great cookbook, plus a bright red Gift Tin filled with delicious, low cholesterol, low salt, high fiber cookies!

# PREFACE

In the early 1960's, my search began for the perfect cookie. My father died at the age of 47, and I discovered I suffered from the same high cholesterol problem and sedentary lifestyle that contributed to his premature death. At that point, I vowed that diet and exercise would become a key part of my life. However, I still had a keen love of great cookies. Thus, I began my search for the perfect cookie: one that was low in cholesterol, high in fiber, had nutritional value and, most of all, great taste.

That initial search began at the University of Michigan in the early 60's, where baking helped pay for school. It followed me through my fellowship in London, England; my surgical residency at the University of Colorado; the war in southeast Asia; and, finally, to the shores of Puget Sound. Along the way, many recipes were collected and created. Most were for cookies. Some were for brownies and quick breads. In the mid 1980's, I joined forces with friend and fellow physician Stephen Yarnall, M.D. to form "Dr. Cookie, Inc." As a cardiologist and fellow cookie lover, he shared my criteria for a quality cookie.

For those who would like to comment on any of my recipes, or would like to learn more about "Dr. Cookie Cookies," I can be contacted by mail through the publisher of this book.

In answer to my many friends who have followed my search, I have compiled this cookbook, dedicated to tasteful and healthful recipes. Although our commercial recipes for "Dr. Cookie" remain a trade secret, many

other wonderful recipes are included in this book. I am
certain you will be pleased with the result. So come now
and be part of that search that began so many years ago.

Dr. Cookie
Marvin Wayne

# FOREWORD
## REALLY About the Author

*Stephen R. Yarnall, M.D., F.A.C.C.*

Marvin Wayne is Dr. **Cookie**, and Dr. Cookie is crazy! Crazy about life! And this book proves it. Who but Marvin would be crazy enough to spend countless hours in search of the *"ultimate cookie"* -- and then write a cookbook on his cookie quest? But more than cookies characterize Dr. Cookie, and more than cookies are in this adventurous book.

As if Emergency Medicine is not challenging enough to *practice*, Marvin travels all over the world *talking* about it. I'm not quite certain if his popularity as a speaker is due to his facts, his style, or his habit of bringing his original "Dr. Cookie cookies" with him. Look for him on your next flight. He always carries his cookies with him. If you're lucky enough to be on one of the airlines serving a Dr. Cookie dessert snack, you'll love it and know that an airline serving a quality cookie must be a quality airline. You wouldn't want to fly on an airplane serving junky cookies, would you?

When Marvin is not flying high in the air, he is often sailing swiftly on the sea. This Type A madman has sailed the Victoria to Maui race and other races, and when he is not in large boats, he loves to windsurf!

He also collects art in his home in Bellingham, Washington, and persuaded my favorite artist, Jody Bergsma, to paint an original Dr. Cookie sweatshirt for me. It's one of a kind, and I love it!

Marvin is a man with a mission. The mission may change from moment to moment, but never doubt there is a purpose! If his energy, good humor, health, and productivity, and zest for life could be put into a recipe, it might read like this: one day of good eating, one day of good exercising, one day of good humor, one day of good friends, one day of work, one day of play: mix thoroughly and enjoy.

I hope that the taste of the recipes in this book can give you a taste of the man who made them, Dr. Cookie himself, Marvin Wayne, M.D.!

Stephen Yarnall, M.D.
F.A.C.C.

# COOKIES

*Advice from the Doctor:*

*Good cookies require love and care.*

*Use only safflower, corn, or soy oil, or margarine. Be sure the brown sugar is as lump free as possible. Use non-stick spray on your pans or cookie sheets, not grease! I've suggested the types of ingredients to use, but feel free to substitute and experiment. That's half the fun.*

*Most of all, don't overcook them.*

*Enjoy!!!*

# Fruit
## Favorites

*Here is a great way to start your cookie trip. This one is tasty the year 'round, but is especially good in the Fall with fresh Washington apples.*

# Old Fashioned Apple Cookies

3/4 cup corn oil margarine
1 1/2 cups brown sugar
1 egg
1/2 cup apple juice
1 cup whole wheat flour
1 cup unbleached white flour
1/2 teaspoon salt (optional)
1 teaspoon baking soda
1/2 teaspoon cloves
1 teaspoon cinnamon
1 cup finely chopped, peeled and cored apples
1 cup raisins
3/4 cup nuts

Mix margarine and sugar. Add egg and juice. Add dry ingredients and mix well. Add apples, nuts, and raisins and mix. Drop by teaspoonfuls onto cookie sheet. Bake at 350° 12-14 minutes. Makes about 4 dozen cookies.

*This recipe even made a banana lover out of me!*

# Banana Surprise Cookies

3/4 cup corn oil margarine
1 cup brown sugar
1 egg
1 cup mashed banana
1 1/2 cups unbleached white flour
1/2 teaspoon baking soda
1/2 teaspoon salt (optional)
1 1/2 cups rolled oats
1 teaspoon cinnamon
1/4 teaspoon nutmeg
1/2 cup nuts (or 1/4 cup nuts plus 1/4 cup wheat germ)

Mix margarine, sugar, egg, and banana. Add dry ingredients. Mix well. Drop by teaspoonfuls onto cookie sheet. Bake at 350° for 12-14 minutes. Makes about 3 1/2 dozen cookies.

*If you like fruit cookies - and who doesn't - here are several recipes that are sheer heaven. Especially good around the holiday season, or spring, or summer, or fall, or ...*

# Pineapple Raisin Cookies

3/4 cup corn oil margarine
1 cup brown sugar
1 egg
3/4 cup crushed pineapple, undrained, in natural juices
1 teaspoon vanilla
2 cups unbleached flour
1 teaspoon baking powder
1/2 teaspoon baking soda
1/2 teaspoon salt (optional)
1/2 cup raisins
1/2 cup nuts

Mix sugar, margarine, eggs, and vanilla. Add raisins and pineapple. Mix well. Add remaining ingredients and mix. Drop by the teaspoonful onto cookie sheet. Bake at 350° for 12-14 minutes. Makes about 3 1/2 - 4 dozen cookies.

*In this recipe and the one following it, you can use your own homemade or store-bought applesauce. You'll get the best results with the unsweetened type. Be careful - tasting the dough can be habit forming.*

# Applesauce Cookies

3/4 cup margarine
1 cup brown sugar
1 cup applesauce - natural unsweetened
1 egg - well beaten
2 cups whole wheat flour (or 1 cup whole wheat plus 1 cup
  unbleached white flour)
1 teaspoon baking soda
1/2 teaspoon salt (optional)
1 teaspoon cinnamon
1/2 teaspoon nutmeg
1/2 teaspoon cloves
1 cup nuts
1 cup raisins

Mix margarine and sugar, and the applesauce and soda. Combine the two mixtures. Add egg, and then the dry ingredients. Drop by teaspoonfuls onto cookie sheet and bake at 350° for 15 minutes. Makes about 4 dozen cookies.

# Oats
# Plus

# Oatmeal Applesauce Cookies

3/4 cup corn oil margarine
1 cup brown sugar
1 cup applesauce - natural unsweetened
1 teaspoon vanilla
1 1/2 cup rolled oats
2 cups unbleached white flour
1/4 teaspoon salt (optional)
1 teaspoon cinnamon
1/2 cup nuts
1/2 cup dates (chopped)
1 egg
1 teaspoon baking soda
1 1/2 cups sunflower seeds (raw)

Mix margarine, sugar, and egg. Add remaining ingredients, mixing as you add. Drop by teaspoonfuls onto cookie sheet. Bake at 350° for 12 minutes. Makes about 4 dozen cookies.

# Oatmeal Raisin Cookies

1 cup unbleached flour
3/4 teaspoon soda
1/2 teaspoon salt (optional)
1 teaspoon cinnamon
1 1/4 cups brown sugar
2 eggs
1 teaspoon vanilla
3/4 cup corn oil margarine
1 cup raisins
2 cups rolled oats
1/2 teaspoon nutmeg

Sift together flour, soda, salt, nutmeg, and cinnamon. Add margarine, sugar, eggs, and vanilla. Beat until smooth. Stir in oats and raisins. Drop by teaspoonfuls onto cookie sheet and bake at 350° for 12-15 minutes. Makes about 3 1/2 to 4 dozen cookies.

# Oatmeal-Date Cookies

1 cup unbleached flour
1/2 teaspoon salt (optional)
1 teaspoon baking soda
1/8 teaspoon ground nutmeg
3/4 cup corn oil margarine
1 1/2 cups brown sugar
1 egg
1/2 cup plain yogurt
1 teaspoon vanilla
2 1/2 cups rolled oats
1 cup chopped, pitted dates

Sift together flour, salt, baking soda, and nutmeg. In a separate bowl, mix margarine and sugar until well blended. Beat in egg, yogurt, and vanilla. Stir in flour mixture. Add oats and dates, mixing well. Drop by tablespoonfuls onto cookie sheet. Bake at 350° for 12-14 minutes. Makes about 4 dozen cookies.

# Oat and Prune Chews

3/4 cup corn oil margarine
1 cup brown sugar
2 eggs, beaten
1 teaspoon vanilla
1 1/2 cups unbleached flour
1 teaspoon soda
1/2 teaspoon salt (optional)
2 cups rolled oats
1 cup finely chopped prunes

Blend margarine and sugar until fluffy. Stir in eggs and vanilla. Mix together flour, soda, and salt. Stir into creamed mixture. Add oats and prunes. Drop by spoonfuls on a cookie sheet. Bake at 350° for 12-14 minutes. Makes about 4 dozen cookies.

*Why do I call these "Nitty Gritty Cookies"? Well, try them. The seedier you make them, the grittier they come out, and the neater they taste.*

# Nitty Gritty Oatmeal Cookies

3/4 cup oil
1 1/2 cups brown sugar
2 eggs
1/4 cup water
1 teaspoon vanilla
1 cup whole wheat flour
1/2 cup unbleached white flour
1 1/2 cups rolled oats
3/4 teaspoon baking soda
3/4 teaspoon baking powder
1 teaspoon cinnamon
1 1/4 cups mixed raw seeds (sunflower, sesame, flax, etc.)
1/2 cup raisins
1/2 teaspoon salt (optional)

Mix sugar, oil, eggs, and vanilla. Add dry ingredients and mix. Add approximately 1/4 cup water to make the dough the right consistency. Add seeds and raisins and mix. Drop by teaspoonfuls onto cookie sheet. Bake at 350° for 12-14 minutes. Makes about 4 dozen cookies.

*I guess you might call this my seedy phase -- here are some more seed cookies!!*

# Oat and Seed Cookies

1/3 cup corn oil
1/2 cup corn oil margarine
1 1/4 cups brown sugar
1 egg, beaten
1 teaspoon vanilla
1/3 cup water
1 cup whole wheat flour
2/3 cup unbleached flour
2 teaspoons baking powder
1/2 teaspoon salt (optional)
1 teaspoon cinnamon
2 cups rolled oats
1 cup raw sunflower seeds
3 teaspoons sesame seeds

Blend margarine, oil, and sugar until fluffy. Stir in egg, vanilla, and water. Mix together flours, baking powder, salt, and cinnamon, and add to the creamed mixture. Stir in oats and seeds. Mix well. Drop by the spoonful onto a cookie sheet and bake in a 350° oven for 12-14 minutes. Makes about 3 1/2 - 4 dozen cookies.

# Sesame-Oat Cookies

1/2 cup corn oil margarine
1 cup brown sugar
1 egg
3 tablespoons buttermilk
3/4 cup sesame seeds
1 1/4 cups rolled oats
3/4 cup raisins
1 1/4 cups unbleached white flour
1/2 teaspoon salt (optional)
1/2 teaspoon baking soda
1/2 teaspoon cinnamon

Blend margarine and sugar. Beat in egg and buttermilk.
Stir in next three ingredients. Mix together remaining ingredients, add and mix well. Drop rounded teaspoonfuls
onto cookie sheet. Flatten slightly. Bake at 350° for 10-12
minutes. Makes about 3 dozen cookies.

# Peanut Butter-Oatmeal Cookies

3/4 cup corn oil margarine
1 1/2 cups brown sugar
1 cup peanut butter (crunchy is best)
2 eggs
1 teaspoon vanilla
2 cups unbleached flour
1 cup rolled oats
1/2 teaspoon salt (optional)
1 teaspoon baking soda

Cream margarine and sugar. Add eggs, peanut butter, and vanilla. Mix well. Stir in remaining dry ingredients. Drop by teaspoonfuls onto cookie sheet. Bake at 350° for 12-15 minutes. Makes about 3 dozen cookies.

# *Carob*
# *Collection*

Carob - not carrot - is like chocolate but much better. It tastes great, and it's better for you. It contains none of the caffeine-like substances found in chocolate. However, for those of you who are true chocolate addicts, chocolate chips can be substituted for carob chips in any of these recipes.

Here is an array of carob cookies, from the basic to the nutty (the cookie - not the baker), to the super, etc., etc. Whether you use carob or chocolate chips, these are some of my best!

# Basic Carob Chip Cookies

1 cup corn oil margarine
2 cups brown sugar
2 eggs
1/2 teaspoon vanilla
2 cups whole wheat flour
1/2 teaspoon baking powder
1 teaspoon salt
3/4 cup carob chips

Mix eggs, sugar and margarine. Add remaining ingredients. Drop by teaspoonfuls onto cookie sheet. Bake at 350° for 12-15 minutes. Makes about 3 dozen cookies.

# Nutty Carob Oatmeal Cookies

3/4 cup corn oil margarine
1 1/2 cups brown sugar
2 eggs
1/2 cup buttermilk
1 teaspoon vanilla
1 1/2 cups unbleached flour
2 cups rolled oats
1/4 teaspoon salt (optional)
1 1/2 cups carob chips
1 cup nuts

Mix margarine, eggs, brown sugar, vanilla, and buttermilk. Add dry ingredients and mix well. Add chips and nuts and mix. Drop by teaspoonfuls onto cookie sheet. Bake at 350° for 12-14 minutes. Makes about 3 1/2 dozen cookies.

# Carob and Coconut Oat Cookies

1/2 cup corn oil margarine
2/3 cup brown sugar
1 egg, beaten
1 teaspoon vanilla
2/3 cup unbleached flour
1 teaspoon baking powder
1/2 teaspoon salt (optional)
1 cup rolled oats
1/2 cup carob chips
1/2 cup shredded, unsweetened coconut
1 tablespoon water

Cream margarine and brown sugar until fluffy. Stir in egg
and vanilla. Mix together flour, baking powder, salt, and
stir into creamed mixture. Add oats, chips, coconut, and
water. Mix well. (Dough will be sticky.) Spread on a
sprayed 8" or 9" pan. Bake at 350° for 20 minutes. Cook
before cutting into squares. Makes about 30 squares.

# Carob Nut Cookies

1 cup unbleached flour
2 tablespoons wheat germ
1/2 teaspoon baking soda
1/2 teaspoon salt (optional)
1/2 cup corn oil margarine
3/4 cup brown sugar
1/2 teaspoon vanilla
1 egg
3/4 cup carob chips
1/2 cup coarsely chopped nuts

Mix dry ingredients.  Cream margarine and sugar together.
Add vanilla and egg, and beat well.  Add dry ingredients
and mix well.  Stir in carob chips and nuts.  Drop by
teaspoonfuls onto cookie sheet.  Bake at 350° for 12
minutes.  Makes about 3 dozen cookies.

# Super Carob Nut Cookies

1 cup corn oil margarine
1 1/2 cups brown sugar
2 eggs
1 teaspoon vanilla
3/4 cup whole wheat flour
3/4 cup unbleached flour
2 tablespoons wheat germ
2 teaspoons baking soda
1/2 teaspoon salt (optional)
1 cup carob chips
1 cup nuts

Mix margarine, sugar, eggs, and vanilla. Add dry ingredients and mix well. Add chips and nuts, and mix well. Spoon onto cookie sheet and flatten slightly. Bake at 350° for 12-14 minutes. Makes about 4 dozen cookies.

*These are great for backpacking, skiing, sailing or just plain good eating!*

# Carob Chip Mountain Bars

1/2 cup unsweetened coconut
1 cup margarine, softened
1 cup sunflower seeds, raw
1/2 cup honey
1/4 cup carob powder (or cocoa if you must)
1/2 cup whole wheat flour
1 egg
1/2 cup chopped walnuts
1 teaspoon vanilla
1/2 cup carob chips for decorating tops

Cream margarine with the coconut. Blend 3/4 cup of sunflower seeds in a blender. Toss the sunflower meal into the margarine mixture along with the remaining seeds, honey, carob powder, flour, oats, egg, walnuts, and vanilla. Mix well. Place on cookie sheet in high mounds. Heap each mound with several carob chips. Bake at 350° for 12 minutes, then you're off to the mountains.

# *Assortments*

*When all else fails, you go for the real thing: chocolate. Like everything else in life, in moderation, it won't hurt you!*

# Simple Chocolate Chip Cookies

1 1/4 cups whole wheat flour
1/2 teaspoon salt (optional)
1 teaspoon baking powder
1/2 cup corn oil margarine
1 teaspoon vanilla
1/2 cup honey
1 egg, beaten
3/4 cup chocolate chips
1/2 cup chopped nuts

Combine margarine, honey, vanilla, and beaten egg. Add dry ingredients, then mix in chocolate chips and nuts. Drop by teaspoonfuls onto cookie sheet. Bake at 350° for 12-14 minutes. Makes about 3 dozen cookies.

# Crunchy Chocolate Cookies

1 cup unbleached flour (or 1/2 cup unbleached white and
       1/2 cup whole wheat)
3 tablespoons cocoa or carob powder
1/2 teaspoon baking soda
1/2 teaspoon baking powder
1/2 cup honey
1/2 cup corn oil margarine
1 egg
1 teaspoon vanilla

Combine flour, cocoa (or carob), baking soda, and baking powder, and mix well. Then combine softened margarine, honey, vanilla, and egg. Combine wet and dry ingredients and mix. Spoon onto cookie sheet. Bake at 350° for 10-12 minutes. Makes about 3 dozen cookies.

*This one will really let the sun shine in!!*

# Sunflower Chocolate Chip Cookies

3/4 cup corn oil margarine, softened
3/4 cup brown sugar
2 eggs
2 tablespoons water
1/2 teaspoon vanilla
1 1/2 cups whole wheat flour (or 3/4 cup unbleached white
    and 3/4 cup whole wheat flour)
1/4 cup nonfat dry milk powder
1/2 teaspoon baking soda
1/2 teaspoon salt (optional)
1 cup chocolate chips
1/2 cup raw sunflower seeds
1/4 cup peanuts, raw

Mix margarine and sugar. Add eggs, water, and vanilla.
Mix flour, dry milk powder, soda, and salt. Add to wet ingredients and mix well. Add chocolate chips, sunflower
seeds, and peanuts. Drop from teaspoon onto cookie
sheet. Bake at 350° for 12-15 minutes. Makes about 3
dozen cookies.

# Poppy Seed Cookies

1 cup honey
2/3 cup oil
2 eggs
1 teaspoon vanilla
1/2 cup milk
2 tablespoons grated orange rind
1/4 cup plus 2 tablespoons poppy seeds
1/2 cup nonfat dry milk powder
2 1/2 cups unbleached flour

Blend all ingredients together.  Dough should be thin.
Drop by the teaspoonful onto a cookie sheet, allowing
space between cookies.  Sprinkle with poppy seeds.  Bake
at 350° for 10-12 minutes.  Makes about 3 dozen cookies.

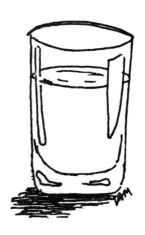

*Borrowed and refined, this is the ultimate granola cookie.*
*You choose the granola, and I promise you a great cookie.*

# The Cerealia Granola Cookie

1 1/4 cup corn oil
1 1/4 cups brown sugar
2 eggs
1 teaspoon vanilla
3/4 cup whole wheat flour
3/4 cup unbleached white flour
1 1/2 cup rolled oats
3/4 cup granola (your choice)
1 teaspoon baking soda
1 1/2 teaspoon salt (optional)
1/2 teaspoon nutmeg
1/2 cup raisins
1 teaspoon cinnamon

Mix oil, sugar, eggs, and vanilla. Add dry ingredients. Add oats and granola. Mix well. Add raisins and mix. Spoon onto cookie sheet and press down. Bake at 350° for 12-15 minutes. Makes about 4 dozen cookies.

# "Coming Through the Rye" Cookies

3/4 cup corn oil margarine
1 cup honey
3/4 cup buttermilk
2 eggs
3 1/2 cups rye flour
1 teaspoon baking powder
1 teaspoon salt
1 tablespoon pumpkin pie spice
1/2 cup raisins
1/2 cup sunflower seeds, raw
1/4 cup sesame seeds

Mix margarine, honey, milk, and eggs. Add remaining ingredients. Drop by teaspoon onto cookie sheet. Bake at 350° for 15 minutes. Makes about 4 dozen cookies.

*Advice from the Doctor:*

*If you want your raisins to be plump, soak them in very hot water for a few minutes, then drain well before adding to any of these recipes.*

# Whole Wheat Fruit Cookies

3/4 cup corn oil
1/2 cup molasses or honey
2 eggs, well beaten
1 teaspoon vanilla
2 cups whole wheat flour
1/8 teaspoon salt (optional)
1/2 cup nuts
1/2 cup raisins
1/4 cup chopped dates
1/4 cup chopped figs

Mix honey, oil, eggs, and vanilla. Add remaining ingredients. If the batter is too stiff, add fruit juice; if too thin, add flour. Drop by teaspoonfuls onto cookie sheet and flatten. Bake at 350° for 12-15 minutes. Makes about 3 dozen cookies.

*I borrowed this old southern favorite from a northern friend of mine.*

# Molasses-Ginger Drops

3/4 cup corn oil margarine, softened
1/3 cup brown sugar
1/2 cup molasses
1 egg
1/4 cup water
1 1/2 cups unbleached flour
1/4 cup nonfat dry milk solids
1/2 cup wheat germ
1 teaspoon baking powder
1 teaspoon ginger
1/2 teaspoon baking soda
1/2 cup raisins (optional)

Mix margarine, sugar, molasses, egg, and water. Add remaining ingredients and mix. Drop by teaspoonfuls onto a cookie sheet. Bake at 350° for 12-14 minutes. Makes about 3 dozen cookies.

# Pumpkin Date Walnut Cookies

1 1/2 cups whole wheat flour
1 teaspoon baking soda
1/2 teaspoon salt (optional)
1/2 teaspoon cinnamon
1/2 teaspoon nutmeg
1/4 teaspoon cloves
1 cup corn oil margarine
1/2 cup honey
1 egg
1 cup puréed pumpkin
1 cup walnuts
1 cup dates, chopped

Stir together dry ingredients and spices. Cream margarine and honey, beat in egg, and stir in pumpkin. Add dry ingredients, then nuts and dates. Mix. Drop by heaping tablespoonfuls onto cookie sheet. Bake at 325° for 12-15 minutes. Makes about 3 dozen cookies.

*When it's zucchini season and you're looking for something to make with them, here is just the treat!*

# Zucchini Drop Cookies

1 cup grated, peeled zucchini
1 teaspoon baking soda
3/4 cup honey
1/2 cup corn oil margarine
1 egg, beaten
2 cups whole wheat flour (or 1 cup whole wheat and 1 cup
      unbleached white flour)
1 teaspoon cinnamon
1/2 teaspoon cloves
1/2 teaspoon nutmeg
1/2 teaspoon salt (optional)
1 cup chopped nuts
1 cup raisins
1/2 cup shredded coconut

Beat together the zucchini, soda, honey, and margarine.
Add egg and beat well. Mix together the flour, cinnamon,
cloves, nutmeg, and salt. Add flour mixture, nuts, raisins,
and coconut to egg mixture. Drop by the teaspoonful onto
baking sheet. Bake at 350° for 12-15 minutes. Makes
about 3 1/2 - 4 dozen cookies.

*Advice from the Doctor:*

*A food processor makes the shredding of zucchini or similar
ingredients a cinch.*

*My wife dislikes peanut butter - but with this recipe, I might make her a peanut butter lover.*

# Peanut Butter Supreme

1/2 cup corn oil
1/2 cup natural peanut butter - crunchy
1 cup brown sugar
1 egg
1 teaspoon vanilla
3 tablespoons buttermilk
1/2 cup nonfat dry milk solids
3/4 cup whole wheat flour
1/4 cup wheat germ
3/4 teaspoon salt (optional)
1/4 teaspoon baking soda
1/4 teaspoon baking powder
1 cup rolled oats
1 cup raisins
3 tablespoons sesame seeds

Mix oil, peanut butter, sugar, egg, vanilla, and buttermilk. Add remaining ingredients, except the sesame seeds. Spoon onto cookie sheet, making fairly large cookies. Sprinkle with sesame seeds. Bake at 350° for 12-15 minutes. Makes about 18-24 cookies.

*The search for the ultimate cookie began to narrow. Here is an early version of Dr. Cookie for the health food purist.*

# Dr. Cookie - For the Purist

3/4 cup oil
1 cup brown sugar
2 eggs
1 teaspoon vanilla
1 cup whole wheat flour
1 cup wheat germ
1/2 teaspoon salt (optional)
2 teaspoons baking soda
3/4 cup carob chips or chocolate chips
1 cup raw sunflower seeds

Mix oil, sugar, eggs, and vanilla. Add dry ingredients and mix well. Mix in carob chips and sunflower seeds. Drop by the teaspoonful onto cookie sheet. Bake at 350° for about 12 minutes. Don't overcook. Voila! The perfect cookie!!

# BROWNIES
# AND
# FRUIT BARS

*Eating these will give you fruit, fiber and the energy to continue baking.*

# Energy Fruit Bars

1/2 cup chopped dates or apricots
1 cup raisins
1/2 cup honey
1/2 cup instant nonfat dry milk
1/2 cup wheat germ
1/3 cup whole wheat flour
1/4 cup bran (raw)
2 cups chopped nuts (or combination of nuts and sesame
        seeds)
2 tablespoons corn oil
1 teaspoon vanilla
3 tablespoons prune juice or apple juice

Combine all the ingredients.  Batter should be thick.
Spread into an 8" pan and bake at 300° for 30-40 minutes,
until firm.  Cut into squares.  Makes about 2 dozen squares.

*I've slipped in a couple of my brownie recipes, just for something different ... and are they good!*

# Better For You Brownies

1/2 cup oil
1 tablespoon molasses
1 cup brown sugar
2 teaspoons vanilla
2 eggs
1/2 cup broken pecans or walnuts
1 cup wheat germ
2/3 cup nonfat powdered milk
1/2 teaspoon baking powder
1/3 cup cocoa or carob powder

Mix together all ingredients except dry milk, baking powder, and carob powder or cocoa. Combine dry milk, baking powder, and carob. Stir mixture into wet ingredients. Spread in an 8" x 8" pan. Bake at 350° for approximately 30 minutes. Remove from pan and cut into bars while warm.

# Carrot Raisin Brownies

1 1/2 cups brown sugar
1/2 cup corn oil margarine, softened
2 eggs
1 teaspoon vanilla
1 1/2 cups flour, unbleached
1/2 teaspoon salt (optional)
1/2 teaspoon baking soda
1/2 teaspoon baking powder
1/2 cup raisins
1 1/2 cups carrots, finely grated
1/2 cup walnuts, chopped

Mix sugar and margarine. Add eggs and vanilla, and beat.
Stir in dry ingredients. Add raisins and carrots. Stir well.
Spread mixture into baking pan, sprinkle with walnuts, and
bake at 350° for about 40 minutes or until toothpick comes
out clean. Allow brownies to cool, then cut into squares.
Enjoy!

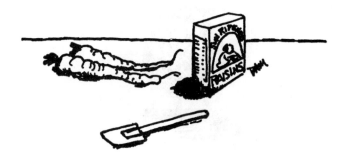

*The Neil Diamond song may go "chunky granola" -- but these are fudgy ones.*

# Granola Fudge Brownies

3/4 cup corn oil margarine
1/3 cup cocoa or carob powder
1 1/2 cups brown sugar
3 eggs
1 cup unbleached flour
1 teaspoon baking powder
1 cup granola cereal - either your own or a commercial
      brand

Mix margarine and sugar.  Add eggs and mix.  Combine cocoa, flour, baking powder and granola.  Add to wet ingredients and mix well.  Spread in 12" x 9" baking pan.  Bake at 350° for 25-30 minutes.  Cool.  Cut into bars.  Makes about 3 dozen.

# Oatmeal-Raisin Brownies

1/3 cup corn oil margarine
3/4 cup plus 2 tablespoons rolled oats
1 cup chocolate chips
1/2 cup brown sugar
2 eggs
1 teaspoon vanilla
3/4 cup unbleached flour
1/2 cup raisins
1/4 teaspoon baking soda
1/4 teaspoon salt (optional)


In pan, melt chocolate chips and margarine. Remove from heat and add sugar, then mix. Beat in eggs and vanilla. Mix flour, oats, raisins, soda and salt. Add to chocolate mixture. Spray a 9" x 9" pan with non-stick. Sprinkle the last two tablespoons of oats into the bottom of the pan. Spoon batter into the pan. Bake at 325° for 30 minutes. Cool. Cut into 24 bars.

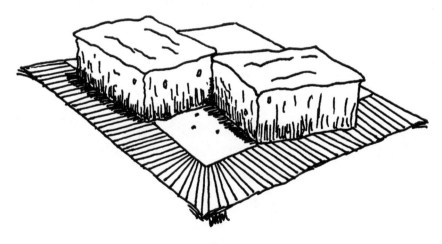

# QUICK BREADS

These are all quick breads. They, like great cookies, require love, care and good ingredients.

Some of these are so good they may make you forget "the glass of wine and thou."

*Like with the cookies, we begin with the apple, just as Adam
& Eve did. (I'm not sure what they have to do with bread,
but it sounded prosaic.)*

# Apple Bread

3/4 cup oil
1 cup honey
3 eggs
1 tablespoon buttermilk
1 teaspoon vanilla
3 cups whole wheat flour
1/2 teaspoon salt (optional)
1 1/2 teaspoon baking soda
1 teaspoon cinnamon
1/2 teaspoon nutmeg
2 1/2 cups chopped apples (about 3 large)

Combine oil and honey, add flour and salt, and mix. Dis-
solve baking soda in buttermilk, add to above, and mix
well. Mix in vanilla, cinnamon, and nutmeg. Stir in
chopped apples. Pour into two 9"x5" loaf pans. Bake at
325° for one hour.

*Advice from the Doctor:*

*Spraying non-stick on cookie sheets and in loaf pans
eliminates the need for greasing, and makes clean up easier
too. In most cases, a 9"x5" loaf pan will work best.*

# Applesauce Spice Loaf

1/2 cup oil
1 1/4 cup honey
2 eggs
1/2 cup water
1 1/2 cups applesauce, natural unsweetened
2 1/2 cups unbleached flour
1/2 teaspoon salt (optional)
1 1/2 teaspoon baking soda
1/4 teaspoon baking powder
3/4 teaspoon cinnamon
1/2 teaspoon cloves
1/2 teaspoon allspice
1 cup raisins
1/2 cup chopped walnuts

Mix oil, honey, applesauce, and water. Mix dry ingredients, add to above mixture, and beat 2 minutes. Add eggs and beat two more minutes. Stir in raisins and nuts. Pour batter into two 9" x 5" loaf pans sprayed with nonstick. Bake at 350° for 55-60 minutes.

# Banana Blueberry Bread

2/3 cup oil
1 cup honey
2 eggs
3 cups unbleached flour
4 teaspoons baking powder
1/2 teaspoon salt (optional)
1 cup rolled oats
2 cups mashed bananas
1 cup fresh or frozen blueberries

Mix oil, honey, eggs, and bananas. Add dry ingredients, and mix well. Gently stir in blueberries. Pour into 2 loaf pans. Bake at 350° for 50-60 minutes. Store one day before eating.

*Since I'm not a great lover of bananas, why do I develop two banana breads? Simple: they taste great.*

# Basic Banana Bread

1/2 cup oil
1/2 cup honey
1 egg
1/4 cup buttermilk
1 cup whole wheat flour
1/2 cup unbleached flour
1 teaspoon baking soda
1/2 teaspoon salt (optional)
1 1/4 cups mashed ripe bananas
1 teaspoon vanilla
1 cup walnuts

Mix oil, honey, and eggs. Alternately add mixture of bananas, milk and vanilla, and mixture of dry ingredients. Pour into 9" x 5" loaf pan and bake at 350° for 50-60 minutes.

*Since the blueberries were so good with the bananas, why not with a little orange flavor?*

# Blueberry Orange Nut Bread

1/2 cup oil
1/2 cup honey
2 eggs
1/2 cup buttermilk
2/3 cup orange juice
3 cups unbleached flour
1 tablespoon baking powder
1/4 teaspoon baking soda
1/2 teaspoon salt (optional)
1 tablespoon grated orange peel
1 cup fresh or frozen blueberries
1/2 cup nuts

Mix eggs, honey, milk, juice and oil. Add dry ingredients and mix well. Gently stir in blueberries and nuts. Pour into two loaf pans. Bake at 350° for 60 minutes. Store one day before eating.

*These have to be two of the neatest fruit breads around. Try them and see if you don't agree.*

# Mosaic Fruit Bread

1/2 cup oil
1 cup honey
4 eggs
2 teaspoons vanilla
1 1/2 cups unbleached flour
1 teaspoon baking powder
1/2 teaspoon salt (optional)
1 pound pitted dates, chopped
1 1/2 pounds dried apricots, chopped
3 cups chopped walnuts

Mix oil, honey, eggs, and vanilla. Add dry ingredients and mix well. Mix in fruit and nuts. Pour into 2 loaf pans. Bake at 350° for about one hour. Cool. Better if served the next day.

# Nutty Date Loaf

2 tablespoons oil
1/2 cup honey
1 egg
1 cup hot water
1/2 teaspoon vanilla
1 1/4 cups unbleached flour
1 teaspoon baking powder
1 teaspoon baking soda
1/2 teaspoon salt (optional)
1 teaspoon cinnamon
1 cup chopped dates
1/2 cup raisins
1/2 cup walnuts

Mix oil, vanilla, honey, egg, and water. Add dry ingredients and mix well. Mix in fruit and nuts. Pour into loaf pan. Bake at 350° for about 1 hour.

*Advice from the Doctor:*

*Checking for doneness by using a toothpick, while a bit primitive, is still a reliable way to keep from over or under cooking a bread recipe.*

*"Yogurt bread?" you cry in exclamation! Yes, yogurt bread --
one of the best breads I've ever eaten. It's good for you, too.*

# Yogurt Bread

1/2 cup molasses
2 cups low-fat plain yogurt
2 cups whole wheat flour
1/2 cup unbleached flour
1 teaspoon salt (optional)
1 teaspoon baking soda
1 cup raisins
1/2 cup chopped walnuts

Mix yogurt and molasses. Mix remaining ingredients and
then add to yogurt and molasses. Pour into loaf pans and
bake at 350° for about 1 hour. Cool 10 minutes and
remove from pans. Store in refrigerator for 1-2 days
before eating.

*A treat, no trick, is this Halloween Pumpkin Bread -- fresh from the "Great Pumpkin's" own hand.*

# Halloween Pumpkin Bread

1 cup oil
1 cup brown sugar
3 eggs
1 cup honey
3 cups pumpkin puree (that is, mashed pumpkin)
2 cups unbleached flour
2 cups whole wheat flour
1/2 cup wheat germ
4 teaspoons baking soda
1 teaspoon salt (optional)
1 teaspoon cinnamon
1 teaspoon cloves
1 cup chopped dates
1 cup walnuts

Mix honey, oil, sugar, pumpkin, and eggs. Add dry ingredients and mix well. Stir in walnuts and dates. Bake in three 8 1/2" x 4 1/2" pans at 350° for 1 hour. Cool 20 minutes before removing from pans.

*You won't have to travel to the islands to love this one.*

# Hawaiian Bread

1/3 cup oil
1/2 cup honey
2 eggs
1 can (8 1/4 ounce) crushed pineapple in its own juice
2 1/2 cups unbleached flour
1 tablespoon baking powder
1 teaspoon salt (optional)
1 teaspoon grated lemon peel
1/2 cup walnuts

Mix honey, eggs, oil, and pineapple with juice. Add dry ingredients and mix well. Pour into a 9"x5" loaf pan. Bake at 350° for 1 hour, then grab a lei and eat.

*What would a cookbook be without a zucchini bread recipe?*
*Here are several of mine . . . they get better and better!!!*

# Zucchini Bread

1/2 cup oil
1/2 cup honey
2 eggs
1 cup grated, unpeeled zucchini, drained
1/2 teaspoon orange extract
1 1/2 cups unbleached flour
2 teaspoons baking powder
1/2 teaspoon baking soda
1 teaspoon grated lemon peel
1/8 teaspoon nutmeg
1/8 teaspoon ginger
1/2 cup nuts

Mix oil, honey, eggs, lemon peel, and orange extract. Add dry ingredients and zucchini alternately, and mix. Add nuts and mix well. Pour into loaf pan. Bake at 350° for 55-60 minutes. Cool in pan 15 minutes before removing.

*A gift from a good friend, this recipe is my favorite zucchini bread!!*

# Zucchini Maple Bread

3 eggs
1 cup brown sugar
1 cup sugar
1 cup corn oil
1 tablespoon maple flavoring
2 cups shredded zucchini
2 1/2 cups flour (1 1/4 cup whole wheat,
     1 1/4 cup unbleached flour)
1/2 cup wheat germ
2 teaspoons baking soda
1 teaspoon salt
1/2 teaspoon baking powder
1 cups nuts
1 cup raisins
1/3 cup sesame seeds
Extra sesame seeds to sprinkle

Mix eggs, sugar, oil, and maple flavoring. Add dry ingredients. Lastly, mix in zucchini, nuts, raisins, and seeds. Sprinkle top with extra seeds and bake at 350° for 1 hour. Makes great muffins, too!

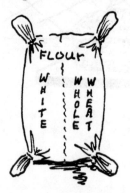

# Zucchini Pineapple Bread

3 eggs
1 cup oil
1 cup brown sugar
1/2 cup honey
2 teaspoons vanilla
2 cups shredded zucchini
1 can (8 1/4 ounce) well-drained crushed pineapple
3 cups unbleached flour
1 teaspoon baking soda
1 teaspoon salt (optional)
3/4 teaspoon baking powder
2 teaspoons cinnamon
3/4 teaspoon nutmeg
3/4 teaspoon ginger
1 cup walnuts
1 cup raisins

Beat eggs, add oil, honey, and sugar. Add pineapple and dry ingredients. Mix in walnuts, raisins, and zucchini by hand. Bake at 350° for 1 hour. Cool for 20 minutes before removing from pan.

# Quick Wheat Germ Zucchini Bread

1 cup wheat germ
1/2 cup sunflower seeds or chopped almonds
1 1/4 cups whole wheat flour
1 tablespoon baking powder
1/2 teaspoon salt (optional)
3/4 cup grated zucchini
1/3 cup honey
3/4 cup milk (buttermilk is my favorite)
1 egg

Combine dry ingredients. Combine honey, milk, and egg. Mix well. Mix the two together until moistened. Spread batter in pan (9-inch round is best). Bake at 375° for 30 minutes, or until toothpick inserted into center comes out clean. Cool in pan for 5 to 10 minutes. Remove from pan.

*This one is truly plum good!!*

# Plum Oatmeal Bread

2 cups unbleached flour
3/4 cup brown sugar
1 tablespoon baking powder
1/2 teaspoon salt (optional)
1/2 teaspoon baking soda
1/2 teaspoon cinnamon
1 cup oatmeal
1 cup diced purple plums
2 eggs
1 cup milk
1/2 cup oil

Mix oil, eggs, sugar, and milk. Add dry ingredients. Mix until just moistened. Add plums and mix by hand. Bake in loaf pan at 350° for 1 hour. Cool in pan 10 minutes before removing. Makes great muffins, too. (Cook 20-25 minutes for muffins.) It's even better the second day!

*Here are two very different breads for you to try.*

# Honey-Oat Carrot Loaf

2 1/4 cups unbleached flour
5 teaspoons baking powder
1/2 teaspoon salt (optional)
1/2 teaspoon ginger
1 1/2 teaspoons cinnamon
1 cup oats
3 large eggs
2/3 cup honey
1/2 cup corn oil
1/2 cup brown sugar
2 cups carrots, pared, shredded, and lightly packed
2/3 cup walnuts or pecans, chopped

Mix flour, baking powder, salt, ginger, and cinnamon. Stir in oats. Beat eggs, honey, oil, and sugar until blended. Add flour mixture. Stir until dry ingredients are moistened, Sir in carrots and nuts. Turn into 9"x5"x3" loaf pan. Bake at 325° until toothpick comes out clean (about one hour and fifteen minutes).

# Oats 'N Orange Bread

2 cups unbleached flour (or 1 cup unbleached flour plus 1
        cup whole wheat flour)
1/4 cup brown sugar
1/3 cup honey
1/2 teaspoon baking soda
1 1/2 cups oats
1 orange, rind and sections
2 eggs, beaten
1 tablespoon oil
1 cup water
1 tablespoon brown sugar

Mix dry ingredients.  Mix 1 tablespoon sugar with grated
orange rind and diced sections.  Add oil, sugar, honey,
water, and the orange mixture to the beaten eggs.  Combine with flour mixture and pour into 1 1/2 quart casserole
dish.  Let stand for 10 minutes, then bake at 350° for 55
minutes.

*From the search for the perfect cookie to the perfect quick bread -- here's my entry in that sweepstakes.*

# Honey Pear Bread

1/3 cup oil
2/3 cup brown sugar
1/2 cup honey
2 eggs
1/4 cup water
2 tablespoons lemon juice
3/4 teaspoon vanilla
1 1/4 cups unbleached flour
1/2 cup whole wheat flour
2 teaspoons baking soda
1 teaspoon salt
1 teaspoon grated lemon peel
3/4 teaspoon cinnamon
1/4 teaspoon cloves
1 cup diced pear with skin (about 2 pears)
1/2 cup chopped nuts
1/2 cup raisins

Beat eggs until foamy. Add oil, sugar, honey, lemon juice, lemon peel, water, and vanilla to the eggs. Beat until blended. Mix dry ingredients and add to above. Stir in nuts, pear, and raisins. Pour into loaf pan. Bake at 315° for 50-60 minutes. Tastes better after it's been stored in the refrigerator overnight.

# DR. COOKIE'S DIET DICTUM
## Stephen R. Yarnall, M.D., F.A.C.C.

People pay an incredible amount for bad food, become obese, and then pay an even more incredible amount for poor advice, fad diets, and diet pills. The most tragic costs are the health consequences of poor nutrition and bad eating habits. But rather than play "trivial pursuits" with various weight loss centers and diets, discussing the failings of each, let me suggest a few principles for reaching and maintaining fitness.

1. *Know thyself* -- be aware of your body's unique composition and needs.

Body weight is an important gauge of health. Know your weight and what your best weight should be. If you are in doubt, measure your body fat and know your body composition. Determine your fitness with a treadmill test, or at least know how much exercise you can do without discomfort. Keep your body balanced with proper amounts of sleep and exercise, and maintain a healthy weight.

Regulate your body's organ functions. Have your chemistries tested every year or so by your physician. These tests evaluate the functioning of your liver, kidney, and thyroid. They also determine your cholesterol level, blood count, blood sugar level, and blood pressure.

If you have high blood pressure or kidney problems, you should consider adjusting your diet. Limit salt and cholesterol intake. Experiment with changes in your diet to see how much you should limit cholesterol versus other fats. You may want to pay particular attention to eggs and red meat, both being notoriously high in cholesterol.

You should also be aware of how your body reacts to different foods. Everyone's system is unique, and what one person can eat with no adverse effects, another person can have a severe reaction to. Milk, for example, is a problem food for many adults. People with an intestinal lactase deficiency experience gas, bloating, fatigue, abdominal pains, and diarrhea when they drink milk. They are simply unable to digest it.

Evaluate your individual condition and determine how diet, exercise, and stress can be modified to improve any problems you have. This is particularly important if you suffer from any chronic conditions.

Having said all this, let me continue with generalizations about sensible eating and nutrition.

2. *Eat breakfast.* This second dictum is critical to anyone who wishes to be healthy. Good breakfast eaters start the day with a burst of nutrition.

The ideal breakfast is a whole grain cereal with milk and fresh fruit. Oatmeal or another high-fiber, sugarless cereal is best. And the milk should be either one-percent or skim. Two-percent milk is two percent fat by weight, but is actually 38 percent fat by calories. This makes it a high-fat product.

If you have an elevated cholesterol level or any bowel problems, I recommend adding one-third cup of oat bran to your cereal. It is the best addition you can make to your diet for lowering cholesterol levels and regulating bowel functions. You can get oat bran in bulk form from health stores for a remarkably low price.

Occasional eggs for breakfast may be a nice variation, assuming that your blood cholesterol is within normal limits, or if you have determined that eggs do not affect your cholesterol level. Have the eggs poached or boiled rather than fried, as frying adds extra fat to the meal.

Avoid eating your eggs with bacon, sausage, or ham, however good they may taste. These breakfast meats rate high on my list of bad-for-you foods. Have whole-wheat toast instead, either dry or with one teaspoon of honey, jam, or apple butter. Stay away from the margarine and butter and you'll save pounds of fat per year.

It is also an excellent idea to include fluid with breakfast. Your body has lost on the average of two pounds, or one quart of fluid during the night. This needs to be replaced.

Hot water is an excellent drink and is good not only with breakfast, but as a snack when other people are having a "coffee break." Remember, too, that soda water is also an excellent beverage with no calories. Add a bit of lemon for taste if you choose.

Many people enjoy a cup of coffee with breakfast. Have some if you like it and if you do not have any caffeine problems. If caffeine does affect you, consider switching to a decaffeinated coffee.

Caffeine varies in its effect on individuals, as does any drug. It can stimulate appetite, give you sweaty palms or palpitations, create nervousness, raise your blood pressure, and alter your sleep even twelve hours or more after the noticeable effects from the morning cup have worn off. I believe this happens because it acts like a swing: its keeps you going all day with ups and downs and withdrawals. This makes you feel fatigued, so you become hungry, seeking food to restore energy.

Another popular breakfast drink is fruit juice. Drink four ounces or so of it several days a week. But don't feel compelled to drink it daily, as most commercial fruit juice is sugar water with vitamin C. It is not intrinsically good, particularly if you need to limit calories. Whole fruit is much better.

Whole fruit also makes a great afternoon snack.

3. *Eat a good lunch.* Make it the largest meal of the day. But don't get crazy with your choices. Salad with a low-cal dressing or a small amount of your favorite dressing is an excellent luncheon. Just don't smother it with cheese, which is a high-fat, high-salt product.

Another good choice for lunch, which is my favorite, is a tuna sandwich made on whole wheat or 7-grain bread. I use mustard instead of butter, along with lots of lettuce, sprouts, and tomatoes. When I want to control my weight I have half a sandwich instead of a whole one, and simply load on more lettuce.

Soups are good. Just be aware that canned varieties are high in salt. And vegetables, raw or cooked, are excel-

lent.  For your drink, iced tea, water, or herb tea is good.
Three times a week treat yourself to an entree-type lunch
with some fancy recipe that pleases your palate.  After all,
this is not a discussion of masochism, but a discussion of
moderation.

4.  *Choose wise afternoon snacks.*  Naturally, we recom-
    mend a Dr. Cookie or fresh fruit.  It's certainly okay to
    have a doughnut now and then, but a Dr. Cookie is a
    more nutritious choice.  Even Cheerios or other dry
    cereal can be used as a snack food, instead of the
    heavily-salted and fat-laden snacks usually eaten.

It's important to stay hydrated, so have something to
drink, too.  Remember that water is better than coffee.

Ideally, we should take a siesta at this time of day, but
our culture is much too Type A for that.  So take a little exercise break instead.  Even a few minutes of stretching and
strolling can replace senseless calories.

5.  *Enjoy a good dinner.*  But get in a little exercise first.
    This will not only make you feel less tired and improve
    your spirits, it will also prevent your eating out of
    boredom and fatigue.  Some people like to have a drink
    before dinner, too.  Certainly one beer, a glass of wine,
    or a single drink now and then has been shown to be
    okay for most individuals.  However, you should
    evaluate for yourself if you have a problem with addic-
    tion or sensitivity to alcohol.

An excellent dinner could include vegetables, rice, or
potatoes.  Try the potatoes with a low-calorie dressing or
yogurt.  Gravy is forbidden in our house except on

Thanksgiving and one or two other occasions during the year.

If you like red meat, stir-fry it with low amounts of vegetable oil and lots of vegetables. It is possible to keep red meat from being a dietary problem.

If you have a weight problem, you might want to have for supper the same thing that you had for breakfast. Breakfast cereals are wonderful for the evening meal anyway.

6. *Be Dr. Cookie crazy.*

So you want to try a crazy diet for a short time before becoming sensible? Here's Dr. Cookie's radical cookie diet. It should end your binge and result in some radical weight loss.

For breakfast, eat one or two Dr. Cookies along with a whole orange or grapefruit, and two cups of hot water or herb tea. Have a cookie and/or a piece of fruit and two more cups of hot water or herb tea in mid-morning. For lunch, have a large salad and/or yogurt, and/or cottage cheese. Include fresh fruit and a Dr. Cookie. Drink two more cups of herb tea, hot water, or cold water with a bit of lemon added.

When it's time for an afternoon snack, exercise a little, and eat something similar to what you had for your morning snack.

Have a bowl of soup or cereal for supper. If you choose cereal, have it with skim or one-percent milk, fresh fruit, one-third cup of oat bran, and one teaspoon of honey. Then for dessert or an evening snack, have another Dr. Cookie and more hot water, iced lemon water, or sparkling soda water.

This diet would surely lead to some type of unidentified malnutrition if continued for more than a couple of weeks. But followed for a short time, it provides a fast start of weight loss. It's also a break from your usual habits and fixed ideas about what you think you have to do, and how you think you have to eat.

The clue to Dr. Cookie's radical cookie diet is the water, high fiber content of the foods, and, most importantly, the monotony. If you get used to eating the same thing every meal, every day for a week or more, you will find that there are other things in life more interesting than eating. And the concept of eating breakfast food for dinner, rather than for breakfast, helps break habits and retrain your body. That way, you can get back to some sensible limitations when you're off the radical or monotonous diet.

7. *The final dictum is: Eat Dr. Cookies*! The commercially-available cookies and those in this book provide a balance for snacks, treats, and desserts. And as stressed in the Dr. Cookie diet section, Dr. Cookies can play an important role in weight loss diets. So consider all the dictums in context and choose health instead of whatever else is second best!